Walrus

Lee Waters

OXFORD
UNIVERSITY PRESS

Here is a walrus.

Here is a walrus
with tusks.

Here is a walrus
with big tusks.

Here is a walrus
with whiskers.

Here is a walrus
with big whiskers.

Here is a walrus.

tusks

flipper

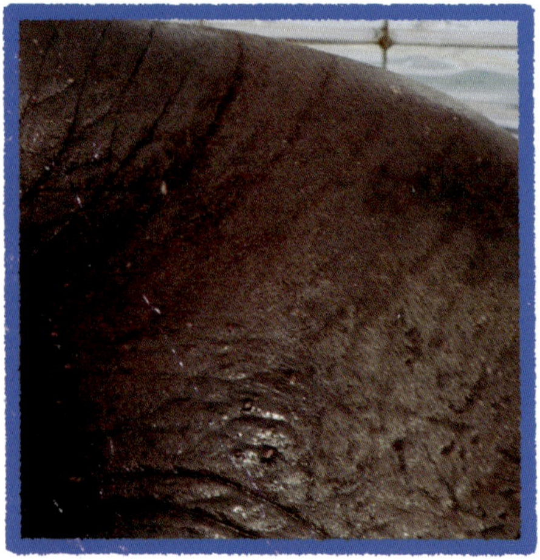

skin

whiskers